HOW GOD HEALED ME

DOMONIQUE HARDISON-HADLEY

HOW GOD HEALED ME

DOMONIQUE HARDISON-HADLEY

How God Healed Me

By: Domonique Hardison-Hadley

ISBN:

DEDICATION

I want to thank my Lord and Savior Jesus Christ for keeping me and allowing me to share this with you. If it wasn't for my relationship with my Father through prayer, I would not have made it. God's grace is sufficient! When I was 15, I made a vow to God when He spared my mother's life, I would serve Him for the rest of my life.

I want to thank my number one supporter. She has been there in every area of my life. When I wanted to quit and leave it all, my mom, Mercedes Hardison, prayed for me the hardest. I want to thank you for pushing me and being a great example to me as a mother, pioneer, and prophetic voice to this nation! Thank you!

To my five beautiful children, thank you for making me the woman I have become. Thank you, Shamira, Johannah, Gabriella, Domonique, and Maudell for loving me beyond my imagination! I love you all!

Thank you to all my supporters I love you so much.

TABLE OF CONTENTS

PREFACE

I remember August 2008, when the time came for me to be put in the hospital. I was home and became very ill. I started throwing up and feeling dizzy, all at the same time, so I decided to go to the hospital to make sure I wasn't pregnant again! Only to find out something worse than being pregnant. LOL!! They gave me some results that would alter every person's life connected to me. This was the day that I found out I had leukemia!

THE SEED

Everything in life starts with a seed. If you want to plant something, it starts with a seed. It must be planted, spiritually and physically, in order to produce a harvest. The life of Domonique Witcher started with a seed.

It was fall of 2008, when a young lady by the name of Domonique Witcher was born in Benton Harbor, MI to the parents of Maudell Hardison and Bill Hadley. At the age of 2, Domonique and her family moved to Minneapolis, MN, where she was raised by her grandparents, Mary and Cecil Gardner. Domonique's mother at that time was strung out on crack cocaine, causing Domonique to be in the home by herself. Domonique's father Bill was living in Chicago, IL. He had a disease called retinopathy, which caused him to become blind at the early age of 45. Domonique grew up in Coon Rapids, MN, where she attended elementary school, middle school, and high school. She was 1 of 12 black people in her graduating class of 380. Domonique had big dreams to move away one day and become a doctor or something great in this world.

At the age of 21, Domonique decided that she was going to get married and move away to Gainesville, FL. While in Gainesville, FL, with their three children, Domonique and her late husband pursued ministry. That is what they were called to do in Florida. Life to Domonique was going well; she was walking in purpose. Do you know the enemy doesn't like it when you are walking in purpose and happy?

THE DIRT

After a seed is put into a pot, the dirt has to be added. We don't think dirt matters, but it does. To see anything grow, it must take root in the dirt and then sprout out of the dirt. Sometimes trials and tribulations feel dirty, but dirt matters. Domonique started getting sick and very nauseated. She was sick to her stomach, throwing up, having chills and dizziness.

The first thing that Dominique thought was, whew, I am pregnant again! Because she was feeling really bad, she decided to take a trip to the hospital to get checked out. She ended up at North Florida Regional Medical Center. She went in and gave her symptoms, and they routinely checked her in by drawing blood and everything else that they do so that they can give a diagnosis. Because she was nauseated and could not keep anything down, they gave her anti-nausea medicine. They had to put another IV in her arm because they needed to draw more blood. Her blood reports showed some abnormality in her red blood cells, white blood cells, and her platelets. Her red blood cells were .4, white blood cells were .6, and her platelets were 00.

The doctor decided that he needed to perform a routine bone marrow biopsy. That would give him the confirmation on what he believed was going on within her body. Domonique began to question the doctor about what was going on. He told her that it looked like she might have some form of leukemia. She immediately gave her consent to have the bone marrow biopsy done. The doctor got his tools and a nurse. He asked Domonique to flip over so her back and backside would be facing him. The nurse stood in front of her. She asked Domonique if she could hold her hands while he was doing what he had to do. Domonique tried to express her feelings, but she really could not do that. She instantly became numb. She didn't know what to feel, how to feel, what to expect, or even what to think. Because Domonique didn't know what to do, she began to pray and ask

God to guide and lead the doctor to take care of her.

The doctor began pressing on her back and found a spot to put the tool he had in his hands. He numbed her and then took a four-to-five-inch needle and injected it into her lower back where her bone was. He told her it would sting a little bit. When he inserted the needle, she felt it go through her skin and into her bone. She felt a burning sensation, which by the way was not fun at all.

She did not stop him because she really needed to find out what was wrong with her. He took the tool that is used for the bone marrow biopsy and poked around to make sure she was numb. Domonique could feel the pressure from the pressing, and she could hear the clinking of his tools. He had to cut the skin to get the tools down into the bone marrow. He was pressing so hard that she could feel it, but it did not hurt at that time. He began to bare down harder, and she felt like her bone was caving in, so she began to scream and holler.

She pleaded for the doctor to get out of her back because it was hurting her. He asked her to bear it a little while longer, and he was taking it out of her because he was almost done. He said he felt they had what they needed. While he was finishing up, the nurse was coaching her by saying, "It's going to be OK, Dominique. Just hold my hand squeeze it as hard as you need to." Domonique used her to relieve some of the pain and frustration that she was feeling and seconds later he was done. He told Domonique he had what he needed, and he was going to send it into the lab. Domonique could feel the blood running down her back and skin.

She could feel him trying to take the towels and stop the bleeding, but at the time she had no platelets to clot her blood. She had blood all in the bed where she was lying. They bandaged her up and cleaned the hospital bed. After all of that, she was kind of weak. She didn't know what to expect from the outcome. After this procedure, the nurse said that she would return when the results came in. Thirty minutes later, the nurse and the doctor came back in the room, and the doctor told Domonique he didn't understand how she was even functioning the way she was functioning. She was confused because she did not know what the doctor meant. He told her that she should be down and out and in a worse condition that she was in. The doctor stated she did not have an immune system, and she needed to be very careful because her body could not fight off anything. If someone with a cold coughed on her or if someone hit her, she would become bruised. If she broke a bone because of her immune system, it may not heal because she was so fragile.

After all of that, he told Domonique that she had acute promyelocytic leukemia (APL). Domonique heard what the doctor stated, but she immediately said, "I appreciate you for doing what we pay for you to do. I appreciate the gift of who you are being the doctor and I am the patient, but I don't receive that because I know a man that is able to heal anything that I go through and anything that I face. He is the one that can heal me."

The doctor asked Domonique about whom this man was. Domonique was not ashamed of the glory of God and stated she was talking about Jesus Christ. She was talking about the man that controls the universe and the one that she prays to everyday. He said everything Domonique was saying was true and he was a believer as well, but he believed that God used doctors to help people. Domonique said to him respectfully that he was definitely right, but she still could not receive what he was saying about her. The doctor told Domonique that she could not go home because they needed to put her in an incubator room for 30 days so that she could get proper treatment. Domonique told him she had a husband and children at home, and there was no possible way that she could stay and get treatment for 30 days. The doctor told her if she was going to leave the hospital that she needed to sign a paper saying that she was leaving against the doctor's will. They were not going to be liable if something happened to Domonique when she left the hospital. He told her honestly that he didn't expect her to wake up the next morning. He also didn't know if she would make it through the night.

Domonique thanked the doctor. She told him God was a Healer, and again she couldn't receive the diagnosis because she would live and not die to declare the glory of the Lord. ("I shall not die, but live, and declare the works of the Lord" Psalm 118:17 KJV) The doctor took the papers again and tried to persuade Domonique to stay in the hospital. After the doctor left, the nurse was baffled but said to Domonique that she had never met anybody with the level of faith that she had. She told her that she needed for her to come to her church and minister. Domonique accepted the invitation and gave her contact information to the doctor.

Domonique walked down the steps, into the elevators, and out the door with the paper still in her hand. She got into her car and drove home. A ten-minute drive became the longest ten minutes she had ever experienced. Part of her was in disbelief, and a part of her was trying to figure out how this had happened to her.

THE PACKING

When you are planting a plant, it is a process before you see the first blooming of a pretty plant. When the dirt is put in the pot and the seed is covered, you have to the pack the dirt in the pot. This process is so the roots can start making a form under the dirt. If the dirt is not packed in the pot, the roots cannot form, and the seed would not harvest a plant.

On Domonique's ride home, part of her questioned God. She asked God how He allowed this to happen, but then there was a spiritual side of her that kept telling her she would get through this trial. After this, she would be a beautiful flower. Holy Spirit on the inside of Domonique told her she would beat this and be well.

Because of the peace Domonique was feeling, she began to take this problem to God for the next seven days. She turned up her prayer life and fasted as well.

She began reflecting on Scriptures in the book of Isaiah, such as *"No weapon that is formed against thee shall prosper; and every tongue that shall rise against thee in judgment thou shalt condemn. This is the heritage of the servants of the Lord, and their righteousness is of me, saith the Lord."* (Isaiah 54:17 KJV)

Other Scriptures she reflected on were *"And when I passed by thee, and saw thee polluted in thine own blood, I said unto thee when thou wast in thy blood, Live; yea, I said unto thee when thou wast in thy blood, Live."*(Ezekiel 16:6 KJV) *"But he was wounded for our transgressions, he was bruised for our iniquities: the chastisement of our peace was upon him; and with his stripes we are healed."* (Isaiah 53:5 KJV)

Domonique kept confessing her healing, so these were the Scriptures that God gave her in the time of distress. Domonique also read *"For in the time of trouble he shall hide me in his pavilion: in the secret of his tabernacle shall he hide me; he shall set me up upon a rock."* (Psalm 27:5 KJV)

Finally, after the drive, she got out of the car, gathered all her bags and prescriptions, and went straight upstairs and sat on the couch. Domonique was still in disbelief. Because of the disbelief, Domonique wanted to call her mom, but her mother was in a halfway house. She had just gotten out of prison, so she couldn't call her directly. Her late husband came over and asked what was going on and what was wrong. It was in that moment that she told him what the doctor had said. He immediately said the devil was lying, and she shook her head in agreement because he was correct. She was going to overcome this. Domonique began to pray strategically about instructions. She asked God how she would get over this and how she was going to get through this. She even asked God how she was going to endure in this process, and the Lord began to encourage her. The Lord told her to "*Be strong and of a good courage, fear not, nor be afraid of them: for the LORD thy God, he it is that doth go with thee; he will not fail thee, nor forsake thee.*" (*Deuteronomy 31:6 KJV*)

After the Lord encouraged Domonique, she began to shed tears. Even though the tears were falling, she could not help but to fall on her face and worship her Creator.

Not only did she worship but began to ask God to forgive her for everything she had done, every mistake, and every mess up. She begged God to forgive her. The spirit of repentance came upon her so heavily.

Domonique did not know how long she had been worshipping because when she got up, it was dark outside.

Domonique got up, went into the shower, and tried to relax to get all of this off her mind. It was exactly three days later when the symptoms began to intensify. She was throwing up almost every 20 minutes. She became weak running back and forth to the bathroom due to vomiting and diarrhea. Her head was so light that she could barely walk by herself. Two days after that, she woke up one night because she felt like she was slobbering on herself. She looked at her pillow, and her pillow was full of blood.

Immediately, she jumped up and ran to the bathroom. She looked in the mirror and opened her mouth. There was a pool of blood coming through her gums. If she would say 'cheese,' she could see the blood imprints around her teeth. She was bleeding so heavily like she was on her period. Domonique continued to endure the pain and the bleeding but later that day sitting at the kitchen table, her sister asked her if she was OK. Domonique stated that she was fine. Her sister asked her why blood was coming out of her ears.

She began to hemorrhage in every place that blood could possibly come out of her. Every place except her eyes and nose began to bleed. She was spitting up so much blood that it filled 20-ounce bottles up within minutes.

A week went past, and it was the same thing.
Domonique's condition worsened because she could
barely walk. She was in so much pain to the point that it
hurt to hold her own head up. She stopped eating and
drinking because the blood was so thick in her mouth.
She went into a state of fasting and praying, and she
prayed to ask God about the right time for her to go and
receive treatment.

Almost two weeks later, she woke up and the Lord
said to her, "Today is the day that you must go."
Domonique and her family prepared for her to go to the
hospital. She had to be carried to the hospital because
she couldn't walk. Her late husband's twin brother
carried her out to the car. He and the mother of his
children took Domonique to the hospital. They took her
to one hospital, and that hospital transferred her to the
cancer unit at Shands Hospital in Gainesville, FL. Two
intensive care units were transporting her. As she was
awaiting to be transferred, she was laying there in the
bed and began to drift off. She told the Lord, "Whatever
you do, don't take me like this." During all of this, her
three-month-old's face began to come before her, and
she began to see her mother, her father, and different
people. It was a slight moment where she blacked out
and her ex-brother-in-law, who was watching her, ran
to her and asked her if she was okay. He was also
shaking the bed and when he shook the bed, I said, "Yes,

I am okay. Let's go!" They transported her to the hospital where it was only cancer patients on the floor, and they began their routine. Day one was a very rough night. She could not sleep due to the nurses had to come in and out of her room every 45 minutes because she was a critical patient. They had to visit often and so they would come in, take vitals, and make her stretch and do different exercises. Then they would give her 45 pills to take. Some days she could not eat or take 45 pills. It was a whole lot for one body to consume. Every time the nurse would give her the medicine, she would tell her to wait. They had to pray over the medicine before Domonique took it.

During this time, she had to have blood transfusions. After taking 45 pills a day, which was a combination of vitamins, chemo medicine, and antibiotics. They were different things to help her body.

Domonique was taking 45 to 47 pills every day. Those two extra pills were Benadryl, and she had to take that before she could have a blood transfusion in case something went wrong with the blood. The nurse would hang the bag of blood and tell her that before she hooked it up to her, let her pray over the blood. She would reach her hand up and touch the bag and pray, "Lord, let this blood that is going to run through her veins be purified by the blood of Jesus, and no weapon formed against her shall be able to prosper. Amen." Domonique was in agreement and said, "Amen." Then she would lay back down and let the nurse do what her job was. Domonique honored Ms. Susie because she was one of the most caring nurses that ever took care of her. Ms. Susie was nice to her family when they came in. She made sure that whatever they needed was there. If they needed food, parking or whatever, she made sure she accommodated. Ms. Susie always checked on Domonique before she went home. She would be her very last patient she would see when she left and the first patient she would see in the morning. She was in the hospital for 30 days.

THE BUD

After a seed has been in the dirt for a while, and it is regularly watered and put in sunlight for it to grow, a bud begins to come up out of the dirt. Domonique began to experience something different. She began to experience God on another level one night. While sleeping, she felt a breeze come through the curtain of the room. It woke her up. She looked around but didn't see anybody. Domonique thought the air conditioner kicked in or something. She laid back down because she didn't see anybody. She laid on her back and started to close her eyes until she felt like there was someone watching her. She lifted her head off the pillow and looked down by her feet. This time it was a little Caucasian boy, maybe the age of seven, was standing there.

Domonique was in awe. The little boy passed her bed and began to go towards the window, and that is when the Holy Ghost quickened Domonique. She realized that the boy was a spirit and not an actual person. She immediately began to pray and tell him to go back to the body he was snatched from. When Domonique said that, he stopped in his tracks, shook his head no, and proceeded to walk. This time Domonique hollered "in the name of Jesus, I command you to go back now! It is not your time yet!" He turned around and went back through the door that he entered.

The very next day when the nurse came in and bathed Domonique, she began to tell the nurse what she experienced the night before. The nurse told Domonique that the little boy that she was talking about died on the night prior. They began to work on him for almost 14-15 minutes to bring him back. She told Domonique that the boy is alive and well, but he is doing better than he ever has since being in the hospital over the past four months. God began to show us miracles in ways that we knew not. *"For I know the thoughts that I think toward you, saith the LORD, thoughts of peace, and not of evil, to give you an expected end."* (Jeremiah 29:11 KJV)

17 *The Bud*

The nurse told Domonique she believed her because she knew she did not leave her hospital room. She was leaving the room but told Domonique God had to show her this because flesh and blood did not show her this. *"And Jesus answered and said unto him, Blessed art thou, Simon Barjona: for flesh and blood hath not revealed it unto thee, but my Father which is in heaven."* (Matthew 16:17 KJV)

Two weeks after this revelation, Domonique was preparing to leave the hospital because her 30 days had come to an end. Her mother came from Minnesota to help her when she was released from the hospital. She took care of Domonique and helped her with the kids. Domonique had to get pick lines in her arm that went up into her heart. Domonique had the pick lines temporarily so that when she went to hospital, she didn't have to keep getting stuck by a needle.

Domonique went to the outpatient clinic every day, Sunday through Friday. This was routine to make sure that her blood levels did not drop into the danger zone. The nurses gave her antibiotics. They would check her blood, weight, and temperature and ask her for a detailed report of what she had eaten that day.

Domonique had gotten an infection in her blood, and it felt like her body was overheating. Her antibodies and her blood were fighting each other, which caused the infection, so the nurse came and gave her Benadryl. It made her sleepy. After the Benadryl, they gave her the antibiotic. Domonique began to feel strange. Her mother was sitting next to her, and she began to scratch and itch. She did not know what was going on and asked her mother what the hospital gave her. Her mom became frantic because Domonique was swollen. She called the nurse over, and the nurse gave her the mirror. Her lips were four sizes bigger; her eye was swollen. Domonique was having an allergic reaction to something. She could hardly breathe, nor could she swallow. Her airway was shutting down, so they began to pump Benadryl into her body. Once the swelling went down, it was an indication that her body was fighting off the infection.

When Domonique went home, she had to be on Percocet 15 and 30's for her pain and when she went into the office, they would shoot her with morphine to make her comfortable. Her body was in so much excruciating pain. It caused her to not to be able to do for herself. She needed a caretaker. About 30 days later, she had to be taken back to the hospital. She had to walk with a cane and her vision turned black. As she rubbed and batted her eyes, her vision left her. She called the nurse, and the nurse instructed for someone to get her to the hospital as soon as possible. Twenty-four hours later, she began to lose her hearing. She could hear very faintly. She again asked God why she was going through this and why did she have to be patient in this process.

THE BEAUTIFUL PLANT

When a seed is planted, it takes time and patience for that plant to grow and become a beautiful flower. We cannot rush the process. Life is the same way. When we have to endure and wait, the process is not easy for us, but it is necessary. If we hold on, the solution will be greater than the problem.

This process with Dominique took a long time. For about two months, she prayed earnestly to ask God to heal her. She prayed for healing and restoration for two solid months. She went into a place of prayer one day and laid down on the bed. She prayed for her sight and her hearing. She asked God to restore them back to their original state. She reminded God that He was a healer and deliverer. She reminded God that He was more than enough. She relied on her faith, and her vision came back. Right after that, her hearing returned. She lifted her hands and told the Lord she was thankful and grateful.

About three weeks after that incident, she was home and was getting ready to get her hair done. She had been wearing a scarf for months. She wouldn't wash her hair; her scalp was really irritated. She took a brush and began to brush her hair. Her hair started to come out. The more she combed or brushed, the more clumps of her hair were coming out.

Domonique began to weep because she had prayed and asked God whatever He did to not let her lose her hair. She did not want to look like what she was going through. She did not want to live this out publicly. She did not want people to know what she was going through. The reason behind that was she wanted to go through in a way that would not bring shame. She was embarrassed. She did not want to go to church looking the way she was looking. She stood in a mirror and cried for almost two hours. She picked up the phone to call her mother. As soon as her mother answered the phone, her mother knew something was wrong.

Domonique told her that her hair was coming out. Domonique was so regretful. (We must learn not to live in regret.) She was so sure that God would honor this request. She kept saying she did not want to look like cancer, and she did not want her hair falling out. The Lord told her to have her brother cut her hair into a fade. She told him, and he brought his clippers so he could do their hair. He probably thought her late husband wanted his hair cut as well.

He came in and greeted everybody and when he greeted Domonique, she greeted him and told him she really needed him to do this for her. He did not understand. Domonique told him that she was sick, and tears welled up in his eyes. She asked him to really listen because he was the only option that she had. She really would love for him to do this because she didn't want to go to the actual barbershop and have to explain to them that she had leukemia and her body was stricken with this disease. She told him that she was praying that God healed her. It took them about ten minutes going back and forth, trying to figure out how they were going to do this, and he finally said OK. He said he would do it with a nice lineup. He removed the scarf, and she showed him all the hair that she was losing. He was just so broken.

Twenty minutes later, she sat down and allowed him to cut her hair. The Lord had given her this strategy so that she would not go bald. She had some irritation of the scalp and things of that nature that were sore; however, she overcame the itching of the scalp.

The Beautiful Plant 22

Domonique overcame her hair being gone for months. She wore an all over even haircut and sometimes she would fix herself up and put on makeup so that she looked like a woman. Domonique went to the store, and there were two African guys. Because she had her makeup on, her hair was cut and she had on jewelry, one of the guys came and kneeled at her feet. He began to say Princess from Ghana. Domonique was looking around, too, for the princess and then realized they were looking around and everybody was staring at her. She was kind of embarrassed because she kept trying to tell them she was not who they thought she was.

This story was not told because Domonique wanted anyone to feel sorry for her. She told this story because there are many people in this world going through the same thing, and they are miserable, embarrassed, and did not expect it to happen to them. The beauty in the story is God is still a healer. Domonique is still here to tell the entire story, and that is a blessing. The process of a seed to a flower is the process from our problem to our solution. We must learn to take our experiences and use them to bless other people. *"And they overcame him by the blood of the Lamb, and by the word of their testimony; and they loved not their lives unto the death."* (*Revelations 12:11 KJV*)

ABOUT THE *Author*

Domonique Hardison-Hadley was born in Benton Harbor Michigan, raised in Minneapolis Minnesota. Domonique grew up in proverty, hearing gun shots, seeing drugs being sold. Raised by her grandparents, never having the fulfillment of being raised in a stable home. At the age of 15 Domonique was introduced to Jesus with the evidence of speaking in tongues. Getting married at the age of 21 for 10 years and being divorced, Domonique manage to make something out of herself. Domonique didn't allow her past to control her future. Domonique is now a entrepreneur of multiple streams of income. She is the CEO of M & D Health Services, CEO of Nique's Collection, CEO of Domonique's Vending Services, Co- Owner of Weave on Wheels, CEO of Domonique's Divine Catering & Chef. She is the Pastor of Faith Workz International, Prophetess, Author, Teacher, Midwife, Intercessor, & Voice to the NATIONS.